MANUEL RIVAS

FROM unknown to unknown

Published by
SMALL STATIONS PRESS
20 Dimitar Manov Street, 1408 Sofia, Bulgaria
You can order books and contact the publisher at
www.smallstations.com

This work has been published with a grant from
the Spanish Dirección General del Libro, Archivos y Bibliotecas, Ministerio de Cultura

GOBIERNO   MINISTERIO
DE ESPAÑA   DE CULTURA

© Manuel Rivas, 2009
Selection and English translation © Jonathan Dunne, 2009
Introduction © John Burnside, 2009
Design © Yana Levieva, 2009

Selection based on the author's collected poems published in Galician as
Do descoñecido ao descoñecido (From Unknown to Unknown) by Espiral
Maior, Coruña, in 2003

The poems 'Serpent with Wings', 'Hunting', 'Shadow' and 'One Missed
Call' appeared in the Winter 2006/7 issue of *Poetry Wales* (editor Robert
Minhinnick); the poems 'Ballad on the Western Beaches', 'Radiophony',
'Vermeer's Milkmaid', 'Red Rose, Proud Rose, Sad Rose', 'The Last
Judgement' and 'Tenderness' appeared in the Spring 2007 issue of *Modern
Poetry in Translation* (editors David and Helen Constantine); the poems
'Joshua Slocum's Trip round the World', 'Blues' and 'One Seventeen'
appeared in the Autumn 2007 issue of *Absinthe* (editor Dwayne Hayes);
the poems 'The English Cemetery', 'Culture', 'Madrid', 'One Eleven', 'One
Twelve' and 'One Sixteen' appeared in the Spring 2009 issue of *Calque*
(editors Steve Dolph and Brandon Holmquest)

This English edition first published in 2009, reprinted in 2017
ISBN 978-954-384-004-5 (paperback original)
ISBN 978-954-384-068-7 (reprint edition)
All rights reserved

MANUEL RIVAS

FROM unknown to unknown

An anthology of poetry by Manuel Rivas

Selected and translated from Galician by Jonathan Dunne
With an introduction by John Burnside

SMALL STATIONS PRESS

CONTENTS

Introduction by *John Burnside* 9

CARNIVAL BOOK (1980)
   To flee from so much natal love 15
   The English Cemetery 16
   Serpent with Wings 19
   Castro de Elviña 21

BALLAD ON THE WESTERN BEACHES (1985)
   Widows of the Living 22
   Ballad on the Western Beaches 23
   Dark Is Life, Dark Death 24
   Incio 26
   Ferrol 27
   On your skin of a boat 29
   I went down to hope and turned over autumn 30
   Lower Miño Days 31
   Promise 33

MOHICANIA (1987)
   Farewell 34
   Joshua Slocum's Trip round the World 35
   Atlantic Avenue 36
   The Lonely Seafarer's Song 37
   The Wood's Army 38
   Mother Earth 39
   Country Suicide 40
   Weight on the Head 41
   Celtic Apocalypse 42

Omen and Legend   43
Blues   44
The Black Earth   45
Radiophony   46
Beirut   47
Letter to a Son   48
Haiku   49
Dakar   50

N O S W A N (1989)
A Thousand   51
She accuses me of having no feelings   52
Can you hear me? I'm in a phone box   54
Yes, I'm still here   55
Power   56
Arzúa: Snowfall of '87   57
Lyric   58
Culture   59
Welcome   60
Terrorism   61
Television   62
Hunting   63
Story   64
Stop   65
Café   66
Cricket   67
New Zealand   68
Childhood   69
Shadow   70
Nationalism   71

DEATH COAST BLUES (1995)
    Babel 72
    A Hot Coffee 73
    Confession 74
    Madrid 75
    Vermeer's Milkmaid 77
    Red Rose, Proud Rose, Sad Rose 78
    The Last Judgement 79
    Hearth 80
    Tenderness 81
    A Man 82
    Botanic Garden 83
    Snooker at the Royal Oak 84
    Unforeseen Destiny 85
    Graveyard 86
    One Eleven 87
    One Twelve 89
    One Sixteen 90
    One Seventeen 91
    Statistic 92
    Message 93
    The River 94
    New Romance of Fin Negan 95

NEW POEMS
    Questions 102
    Graffiti 106
    The Singer's Beret 108
    One Missed Call 111
    Prayer 113
    Practical Guide 116
    Brotherhood 118
    The Enemy's Rap 120

INTRODUCTION

There are those who will tell you that beauty in poetry is out of fashion. Of course, the notion of beauty is odd in itself, especially for those readers who set out to mistake a certain variety of self-limitation for tact, and to see the weary diffidence of the poet who has nothing very interesting to say as a brand of superior irony. It is also the case that this odd beauty is impossible to define; indeed, it can seem that the only way to talk about it is in the negative – we can say, for example, that beauty is neither prettiness nor mere elegance and that, whatever its relationship to 'truth', the claim that 'beauty is truth, truth beauty', suggestive as it might be, is really nothing more than the statement of a tautology. Of course, talking about it may be the very problem: perhaps all we can do is look at the way in which Marianne Moore, say, or Eugenio Montale rediscover language in their poems, or the way in which Rosalía de Castro or Carlos Drummond de Andrade rediscover the world we take for granted, and leave it at that.

No direct comparisons are intended here, but it does seem to me that this process of discovery is central to Manuel Rivas' poems. Again and again, as we listen to the account he gives of the world, we come across the beautiful surprise, the breathtaking renewal of some process or way of seeing we normally take for granted:

They would write letters
with honey and biscuit dawns
and postcards would arrive showing red trams,
watercolour gardens,
cotton poodles
and an absurdly happy couple on Westminster Bridge.

(Widows of the Living)

The revelations in these poems – a revelation that is at once a surprise and a reaffirmation of something known long ago but since un-remembered, like a childhood romance – the discovery – in the old sense of the word – may come from the juxtaposition of the accepted clichés of happiness or beauty and some lyric gift that arrives out of the blue, like those 'honey and biscuit dawns', or it may arise in a single image of extraordinary power and economy, as in the poem 'Country Suicide':

And then there are the earth's dead,
elegant on the branches,
hanging serenely from the dawn on the apple trees,
with their eyes of snow,
like old birds that couldn't emigrate.

Or it may originate in a playful celebration of language, married to a sudden shock of painful or ironic recognition, as in 'Practical Guide', where a hymn to the cultivar names of tree fruits – Granny Smith, Jersey Mac, Williams' Bon Chrétien – ends with the lines:

May the blackbird,
gorged on cherry,
sing a purple song
in the arms of Schneider's Noire.
I lost
the one they called the Beauty,
the most stolen apple in Galicia's orchards.
Only the worm of splendour is left:
the memory of a forbidden laugh.

It is an enormous privilege to have this selection of poems in this attentive and imaginative translation: a privilege and a revelation in itself of the lyric brilliance of a writer that most English-speaking readers have only encountered before now in his novels and stories. Here, we have work from three decades by a poet of enormous range and real emotional and intellectual daring.

Rivas is a poet who understands pain and dread, as well as pleasure and our strange longing not only to be happy but to communicate our happiness, and he is willing to take any risk in the pursuit of his vision – even the risk of making something beautiful, or of saying what he knows to be true without hedging his bets:

Fear, real fear,
comes when the extraterrestrials are
intelligent men
who give themselves away
because they don't have tears
and don't appreciate bitter tastes
such as wine.

(Questions)

Here is a poet who never exercises control for its own sake, but does so in order to accommodate and sustain his passion. His formal concerns arise from a need to make something that is both crafted and spontaneous, artful and immediate. Here, in short, is an essential poet whose work illuminates the world and the condition of those who live it:

The neon shone
with the memory of a river
between the paving-stones.
The kisses were long.
The trams and boats
got lost in them.
What was the message?
Lima Oscar Victor Echo
Again:
Lima Oscar Victor Echo

(One Missed Call)

John Burnside

FROM unknown to unknown

To flee from so much natal love,
so much gnawing.
To walk the slurry of this world,
renounce a bed to lie in.

The English Cemetery

It's almost obligatory to say something of the beauty,
but neither you nor I are in Brañas Verdes,
between Cape Vilano and Tosto,
between Arou and Camariñas.
It rains sand and ash
and I watched the fire stick in the fox's eyes,
the copulation of stud and mare,
the gannet's moment
in the sea-bass' shadow,
the turban of mist
on the peaks where itinerant Hölderlin's
unease blows.

Perhaps in the summer
two or three of us
may think of going to Brañas Verdes,
where I watched the wave's muzzle
kissing reeds.
If we do,
if two or three of us go there,
we may even think of not returning.

On the other side of the dunes
are small oases
with sea pink
and starwort.
A salt garden's silence,
a dumbfounded silence,
the sweet sensation of a secret treasure,
of an underwater hearth,
the flute's hole,
the diving suit,
the octopus sleeping in the comic's grottoes.
One is not indispensable, you know,
and we're thinking of staying.
No one can make somebody else happy
for very long.
Bread is less heavy.
Things are going badly.
What's to be expected
of a cooling star
withered millennia ago?
Paradise, all things considered, is not so interesting.
For sure,
the imagination is not over-exerted
and the brain's capacity is under-used.
Respect, love…

That hasn't existed since they were named.
In short,
this business about Brañas Verdes,
it'd be better to leave it.
We'll come back in the summer.
It doesn't rain in seven colours.
Rimbaud is in Abyssinia,
trading ivory.
Here are photos of Brañas Verdes Valley,
between Cape Vilano and Tosto,
between Arou and Camariñas.
The cassette tape contains echoes of the sea.
In the pockets, shells with strange shapes.
(Leave the rabbit's tail on the coffin:
it's supposed to bring good luck.)

Echoes of the sea,
yes,
strange shapes.

Serpent with Wings

> *The moonlight's brotherly voice in the sacred night*
> Georg Trakl

Nearby, the serpent, the breath.
The fire's coldness in the yellow wheat-fields.
Nearby, the rainbow, the returning rivers.
The samurai in the clearing.
The sword's vertigo.
A rose window shattered in artificial festivities.
And from the earth's core
the song of insects.
A man in the clearing,
under the moon.
Between autumn's breasts,
on the lagoons.
Down below,
in the tile-works' forgotten grottoes.
In the eel's electric eyes.
A little owl sieves the moon
in silence.
The smallest star, there, in the clearing,
tear on the sword's blade.
The nails of boars
in the tunnels of moles.

In the rock crystals,
by the golden hair,
by the gods.
There's a man there, in the clearing,
on the sword's tragic blade,
like the first day.
And a serpent with a seagull's wings.
Serpent
with
a
seagull's
wings.
The goldfinch's emerald psalm
– hey, you, sun, amen!
The dawn.

The seagull beats on the blind seas.
In the wood's ferns, the serpent sleeps.

Castro de Elviña

In the light-waterless suburb,
before Chao of Felisa
and Manolo of Hilario,
before Cordeiro son,
in his embrace of a stower of yearnings,
in the hand writing free
on the city walls,
before my people,
before the four winds,
I solemnly declare
that
This life wants another.

Chiribico lights the first firework.
Ssssssss boom!
One, two, testing, cuuuuumbia!
Welcome, party-goers.
Welcome, future days.
Welcome.

Widows of the Living

They would write letters
with honey and biscuit dawns
and postcards would arrive showing red trams,
watercolour gardens,
cotton poodles
and an absurdly happy couple on Westminster Bridge.

Ballad on the Western Beaches

The ship settles on the shore
and land birds nest on its mast.
With the compass I trace routes on maps of tillage,
hurt by the sky's anger on the seed's weak ribs,
fearful of the flower's drift before inhumane winds.
The ship sleeps on the shore,
the keel's blue imagination covered in brush and rushes,
and the figurehead has a strolling soul.
In the binnacle is kept the book of moons and the rains' needle,
a bottle of old snow liqueur.
A skylark sings on a rusty harpoon,
a blackbird's sigh lashes the cables
and crows on the rudder glimpse lesser death lying alongside.
All set, admiral, for the great journey.

Dark Is Life, Dark Death

These eyes with roots
in the sea's naked breath know.
Born in another time,
before the north's stout,
lords of another window,
drunk with other songs,
prisoners of other judges.
There's nothing certain in the fingers,
the stars' speech is transient
and dreams are weak.
Before beauty air fails
and the heart leaps
because no roads of men
take in the beyond.
Others will be the winds
and at each turn
another silence.
A storm brings
anxiety and happiness
and there are always laments in the dorna-boat's underskirt,
for it's fear that conquers in this land.

In another time,
with icebound lips,
in front of the mounds,
of the dark fire that is a seed's nest,
I'll reveal what I read in the future's old rags.
These tired eyes know,
but they do not want to close.

Incio

Two wars have come and gone,
big ones,
but Incio's chestnut woods are still standing.

Fear and hard-headed wind,
but they're still standing.

Ferrol

for Rafael Bárez

The estuary's silence hurts me
without man's drum.

The sun drinks at the springs,
the light leaps from brook to stream
and childhood, wild-grass mountain rolls.
But the estuary's silence hurts me
without man's drum.

Between peak and sky the sea-eagle goes,
the wake of an unrepentant ship:
nothing to lose in the vast expanse.
But the estuary's silence hurts me
without man's drum.

I think of the north, no hunter
or death-protecting law.
I think of the lives I was not, waiting for me in the north.
But the estuary's silence hurts me
without man's drum.

Happy, and happy times!
I know where to find them.
No one will dance on the ashes of happy times.
But the estuary's silence hurts me
without man's drum.

Without man's drum,
without legend woven next to the fire,
without the tribe's warm breath,
without the god of little ones singing against the dark,
without evil, without goodness,
the estuary's silence hurts me.

On your skin of a boat
lying in the garden,
like an orphan vine in winter skies,
let the children draw the colourful clothes-line,
the coarse house,
a casual window looking like a book rescued from the fire,
and the hanging smoke,
like an open throat,
the writing of a pensive
soul
stretching in the sun.

I went down to hope and turned over autumn,
the pantry and the old liqueur.
Kids' stuff is allowed to me
and, what's more,
long walks ending in a wayside cross,
the unalterable ash in the lips' repertory,
the comedy of paths,
the licentious leisure of stone trades,
jargon invented in the wood
and second words.
I wish I'd grown old before!

Lower Miño Days

for Ánxel Vázquez de la Cruz

A river is like a dear home
Álvaro Cunqueiro

You were the child.
Yours were the orange
and the lemon tree that burnt like first loves.
Yours the alleyways of the moon's city
and the riverside horse's
misty locks.

So it was we watched the wood's ossuaries
floating downstream,
the mountain shadow of whales dreamed
in the smoke of freighters.
So it was our wild steps
took in all the blackbird's territory
and the sweet current of its speech.
So it was the echoes of ash,
the painful sun of the day of fugitives,
had lush bodies
that wound charm around the seas' altar.

In the old law,
everything remains, everything decays.
The half moon sleeps and stabs.
The river descends calm and crazed.
With us holding hands, children,
grown-ups, kings brought low.

Promise

for Isa

Feuerspucker
doucement doucement
the slats of the blind
deuladeu deuladeu deuladeu
moth in the rumba of night
purple rain
La boîte de Pandore
purple rain
doucement
deuladeu
doucement

Farewell

The sea will reach the larder
and sleep its blue-jasmine sleep
for ever in the flask of limbo.
The wood will cut its veins
with a Swiss Army penknife.
The moon will hang itself on a Granny Smith tree.
Man left us some time ago.

Joshua Slocum's Trip round the World

Captain Joshua Slocum built *The Spray* on top of an old cemetery. When he put in place the sloop's timbers, the apple trees were in blossom. In the Nova Scotia summer, cherries fell on *The Spray*'s belly. In winter, the whalers warmed their hands in Joshua's workshop and talked to him of the Arctic, the ice candles on their beards and the burst of spit as it left the mouth like a frozen matchstick. He travelled solo round the world to forget a great love.

Land, from *The Spray*, was just a graveyard.

Atlantic Avenue

I await the sea's revenge.
The sea with a madman's eyes turning on land.
The sea bubbling in the black hole of sarcophagi.
The sea knocking at the city gates.
The sea with dry lips.
The sea covering the distance of a fist.
The sea lonely as a jazz solo.
A blind bird.
A blue horse drinking at the mirrors.
The sea.
Drowning my heart, a deep, electric, ancient fish.
Taking me like an animal dozing on the sand.
Far away from you, against you, the sea.

The Lonely Seafarer's Song

I come from the shipwrecked earth.
The earth is melting,
its toy eyes red with anxiety,
like an asthmatic child.
I come from the drifting earth,
fleeing its protracted shouts and cough.
I come from the defeated earth,
where pained riders lance the clouds' black chest.
I'm leaving the wounded earth,
slipping on porcelain with veins wide open.
Take me, sea, far away, somewhere I do not know.
Wrap me in the salty grove.
Kiss me with your lemony lips.
Protect me like a father.

The Wood's Army

Hand me your words, rain,
and you, wind, such long ideas.
Lend me your brief prayer, river,
and, snow, your white greeting.
Ice, place a serene thought on the window-pane
and let dawn's luminous wings bring it to my lips.
Defend me, lightning;
draw near, sword.
Watch out! People are coming.

Mother Earth

I burnt my lips on your skin of ice,
similar to death's, so deep, your embrace.
I'm leaving, earth.
And I'm leaving so that I can love you.

Country Suicide

And then there are the earth's dead,
elegant on the branches,
hanging serenely from the dawn on the apple trees,
with their eyes of snow,
like old birds that couldn't emigrate.

Weight on the Head

My people have their eyes suspended in formalin.
They gave the living a drink,
they gave the living so much to drink
they burst inside like a useless rifle.
The living were a passing cloud.
I recall it being said:
A youth of stars will arrive.
The women sewed and sewed.
I found them once inside a tapestry,
motionless, with their apple faces,
hemmed in by the waves.
I was the one who looked amazed.
I couldn't see them out:
there they go
with a globe
made of ivy
perched on their heads.

Celtic Apocalypse

One day
fire will head for man's home.
No truce will be given the enemy.
The wood's fiery bodies
will roll to the city gates,
besiege it,
and the city will die a slow,
unreal, liquid death
filmed like fiction
by a neurotic, meticulous
and hard-headed god,
like the tourist's
smoking shadow,
his acrylic footprints,
his vampire kit,
on the way to the site
of archaeological beauty.

Omen and Legend

The horse waters the wind.
So much sea in the sky
blinds the stone's irises.
The river escapes through the child's fingers
with its murmur of a stream
in a silver-foil crib.
The trout nests in the wood,
in the bowl of a fallen wing.
The rider gallops in equestrian statue.
With a toothless guffaw,
running along the top of the walls,
the wind anticipates the epitaph:
Let whoever wants to be god!

And the century will give birth to a colder god.

Blues

Only the night is paradise: men sleep.
Dreams open the windows
and lick their wounds on beaches and riversides.
Dreams sing with frozen throat.
Like slaves, they beat the drums.

The Black Earth

If I speak, I will speak to the earth.
The real earth,
the black earth
where the root takes.
The earth that is trodden on.
The earth that is burnt and nailed.
That huge canvas where man draws his caprice.
Where man is lost and writhes in shadows.
The black earth,
that body of an old whore with tobacco-stained teeth
and bags so blue they're black.
If I speak, I will speak only to her
and I'll speak with my hands,
gently with my nails,
with a lover's passion,
the way wounded boars speak when they glimpse death.
If I speak, I will speak to the earth.
To the earth, that black earth
that spits up springs like blood.

Radiophony

Were death to speak,
were it something more than a smell,
it would make this noise:
that of an oar beating against the skin of the void.
I sometimes think I hear it at sea,
between news items extinguished like lights.
The sea is an old radio,
the embrace of a grandfather who became a poet of silence.
The din of your startled horses reaches here,
the anguished neighs of battle.
Your orders reach here,
your sons' laments,
the creaking of the cage.
It's like a falling guffaw,
the beat of an oar against emptiness.
Songs sometimes reach here,
a dance of silks,
and the sea whirls and whirls like an old mystic.

Beirut

Attic in Coruña,
a home at last,
atop an old mast
on the bay's rebellious suit,
with books, the odd picture, a fern, the bird
and the Paul Gonsalves saxophone.
The boy has gone to sleep,
his arms sticking out.
With the din of a nostalgic machine,
they've collected the rubbish in the street.
That distant dog will bark all night.
Hold me like this,
very tight, so I don't feel.
What's left to fall in Beirut?

Letter to a Son

The father's voice has the sound
of a coin on the ground.
Do not inherit his silences,
his diplomatic weakness,
his cowardly cynicism,
his defeat.
Conquer me.
Beat me.
Run so far I cannot see you.
Leave no trace.
Forget me.
And then, if you've guts,
with knitted brow:
love me.

Haiku

While the children play
in 142 days of rain
I sleep in your arms.

Dakar

If one day I had to go to prison, I should like it to be on Gorée
Nicole Nealey-van de Kerchove

Having gone round the sun a couple of times,
I shall commit the crime of growing old.
I should like then, milord, to go to the island of Gorée,
sentenced to sweeping the beaches
and sleeping under the stars in the House of Slaves.

A Thousand

I've something important to say
now that we've just separated
for good.
I love you.
Scratch me with your nails,
but you should know I was also being sincere
the other a thousand times.

She accuses me of having no feelings
because I talk and talk
or do not talk.
She's going to eat all her nails,
her lofty, scarlet nails.
But I will leave.
I told her so and she laughed indifferently,
but I will leave
or will not leave.
I'll arrive in one of those cities,
not so big as a city,
where the train stops and there's no longer a train,
with nuns who sit on a beer barrel in the station
and thousands of crows cynically waiting for the King
or a movie camera.
A bus leaves that city
that is so old
it has a driver who smokes
and talks to the passengers,
at each corner precisely,
when it rains,

and has been doing so every day for ages,
wipes the windscreen with his hand,
as if we were falling,
it rains inside as well.
And nothing happens,
we arrive when it clears
and it's only dripping on the bus,
everybody soaked except for the locals,
who laugh
or do not laugh.
It's no longer a city or anything,
but there's a boat belly up
and a beach of black sand.
And there's a phone box as well.

Can you hear me? I'm in a phone box.
Yes, well.
No, nothing.
It was raining on the bus.
There's only one bar.
Yes, I have change.
Really? Me too. No, it hasn't run out yet.

Yes, I'm still here.
No, I wasn't thinking.
I was listening, that's all.
I don't know what you were saying. I was listening.
No, it's not a book.
It's the pages of the directory.
Do you know what the code for Ras Al Khaimah is?
You dial 00 plus 971 and then 7 and a number at random,
and you can talk to somebody in Ras.
No, it's not that I'm not listening to you.
I am listening, I only want to listen to you.
But don't ask me what you said.
I can't do two things at the same time,
understand and think about you.
It's so easy to talk to anywhere.
No, please don't hang up.
If you go,
I'll call Ras Al Khaimah
or somewhere.
While you're talking, I'm not cold.

Power

God governed the dog in the Conor Pass
and governed the light as well,
so that the flocks followed the sun,
drawing epigrams of praise on Dingle's slopes,
an old green sewn in stone,
darned in fuchsia with a princess' earrings.
God is in charge there,
but not in Slea Head.
Nobody knows who's in charge on the wild cliffs
of Slea Head.

Arzúa: Snowfall of '87

The world grows old
and it snows.
Black hearts caw
and time pants like a frozen schoolchild.
Time waits by the roadside,
its hands in its pockets
and a heavy skeleton under its arm.
Time has the eyes of a cow.
Time holds the hand of a pregnant woman
in red socks.
The world's eyelids droop.
Wounded flakes settle on its lips.
The hearts howl on the ridge.
Time,
time shelters by the fire,
closes its eyes
and dreams it's over.
The hearts whinny on the icy hills.
The world has cold feet.
Eyes burn in the salty silence.
The hearts cough,
are scared off.
Time escapes on their yellow beak.

Lyric

Like Leopardi,
he enjoyed laughter.
Most of all, the laughter
of country girls in high heels
and print dresses,
on a Sunday, after receiving communion.

Culture

At that hour,
in that pub,
all the old men looked like Samuel Beckett.

Welcome

My father would never say anything,
but he hated it when I came home
with long hair like a woman's.
I would greet him, hi dad,
and he would move his right leg
like someone seeking firm ground on a bed of lilies.

Terrorism

She hated them.
She really thought they were a cancer
and agreed when the president
crushed those insects in front of the microphone.
Everything was going badly because of them.
She would have liked to do it herself,
to crush them with the broom
or flush them down the toilet.
So she called on God in front of the news
when that Palestinian fighter struck her as so beautiful.

Television

At that hour my mother would turn up,
just when the bass of *The Cult*
was strutting his stuff like a Comanche.
I'm a wild hearted son!
My mama,
yawning after mopping the offices of Fénix Español,
would put on her slippers,
sit on the sofa,
sigh deeply
and switch to channel one.
Don't just stand there, go out and do something.
But then the vast Empire State Building
appeared on the screen
and my mother crooned:
Poor woman, having to mop all of that!

Hunting

That morning, the hunting party were a happy babble
in the whitened silence of the woods.
The men were passing round the bottle and the dogs snapping
    at the air.
They cleared a way through gigantic ferns,
swept aside tender forests,
quickened their breath in the short cuts,
and a false trail carried them off in the evening.
Those woods were deserted,
burnt to the core.
Tired and ill at ease,
they returned, scratched by the shadows.
One of them fired into the sky. Then they all did.

Story

I was reading the paper,
and the boy was tossing and turning.
I decided to help him sleep with the story of a horse.
I told him it twice.
Once more, said the boy. Just once.
And powerless to resist,
I watched him leave
on his horse,
across the vast plains.

Stop

He had stopped to drink at the roadside.
What bird is that?
A sparrow, replied the farmer without even looking at it.
It wasn't a sparrow.
They both knew it couldn't be a sparrow.
So he got back in the car,
put on his sunglasses
and drove off without saying goodbye.

Café

He hated waking up.
It sometimes took him hours to come to terms with the world.
So he preferred having breakfast in that roadside café
where nobody was helpful.
The customers were cornered creatures
with hangovers in their eyes
and the proprietor poured coffee over the cup without apologising.
But then he weighed more than eighteen stone.
The premises were sold.
The new owner asked questions with a smile.
And he decided to stop going.

Cricket

He wanted to show his children how to catch a cricket.
You have to crawl furtively, like a cat,
into the sun, with your shadow behind you.
In its hole you have to poke it with a straw
and swipe it when it comes out.
And so it was he caught a cricket,
descended from singing mole-crickets,
and made his kids happy for almost a minute.
He carried it in a jar with clover leaves
and the cricket sang all day
and at night,
when the children were asleep,
the cricket still sang.
He watched it through the glass.
It had a strange head,
magnificent and ugly,
like that of an armoured samurai
or futuristic hero.
He took down the bags of rubbish together with the jar.
And there the singing cricket remained,
on the suburban pavement,
at the hour people measure their steps.

New Zealand

That night the radio ham
made contact with the Antipodes.
He was in the Sisargas, by the lighthouse,
under a sky of stars and tardy seagulls.
The valley of the world was asleep.
The man had drunk from the Irish hip-flask
he kept in the tool-box
and felt himself a happy owner of space and time.
He had left everything at home in order, so he believed,
and his enemies died in August.
And now he had made contact with the Antipodes.
He gave his call-sign in Greek letters
and in English asked how it was going.
There was a long silence in New Zealand.
Somebody was there and could be heard thinking.
He repeated his call-sign and again asked how it was going.
Finally a woman's voice answered, Well,
and he breathed a sigh of relief.

Childhood

I dropped the sugar jar
and a glass splinter stuck in my forearm,
but while I cried I ate the sugar.
A year later I started school.
And blood tasted sweet to me,
sweet like tears.

Shadow

Somebody behind, I know.
The hunter without swing,
between prison and lighthouse.
Somebody behind, I know.
I am, and am not, afraid of him.

Nationalism

Down with all nations,
said the kind of beggar.
All of them?
Yes, all.
All except the one
that gives good shade.

Babel

Birds emerging from the phosphorescence.
Flakes of rainbow skin.
Apples of blood in the basket of mist.
Jet hearts pinging on the tiles.
Gorse flowers,
winter sparks,
eyes of nothing,
eternal hinges.
Words,
beads of the poor man they call Abaddon,
king, angel of the bottomless pit:
Thank you, Lord, for that curse!

A Hot Coffee

Give me an honourable sword to lay me down,
said the apple tree,
because I'm bloodless.
I don't want men hanging their jackets
on the stumps of my arms.
Give me a clear day,
said the cockerel.
Or else lamp and moth
to wake a story.
And give me a white lie,
said the people,
a feather pillow on which to alight.
Give me a hot coffee,
said the devil,
to stay awake this night.

Confession

I came out of the mouth of the Most High, says the river.
I'm a tale, said the alder,
of birds and clogs.
I'm a butterfly hunter, said the lily.
I'm a witch's dagger, says the trout.
I'm Hamlet's pain, says the salmon.
And I'm a nostalgic coin, points out the sun.
What are you looking at!
I'm an Arctic tern,
says the man.
I'm just here for the winter.

Madrid

I won't throw a fistful of my earth against anyone.
Besides, I don't have any fresh earth.
I'm as empty as a TV-less old man.
If you want to be alone in the city,
go to a place that talks of Spanish culture
amid the dazed madness of the statues.
You'll say all men love one land
be it an emerald isle,
a cabbage patch next to the rubbish
or a garret on the border.
Right. Well,
today I'm all men.
That feeling,
such a primary feeling,
goes to my head
like smoke from the dry leaves
the gardener burns.
Madrid,
Madrid in autumn
smells of all lands,
all exiles.

People trailing a late train in the iris,
a tray of apples,
a pomegranate,
geraniums behind bars,
the thistle's white flower.
Unless you look in the eyes,
you'll never know of autumn in Madrid,
the dazed gaze of the barbarian kings' statues
missing the birch forests.
I was one of them,
one of those fierce, lonely kings
devouring sparrows and dry leaves.
My country was a bird of smoke
rising from an ember of the Prado
in the Avenue of Museums.
How I loved you both!
Madrid in autumn,
needy capital of an empire
of harvesters of leaves.
And you, my earth,
gauzy mist
in the statues' iris.

Vermeer's Milkmaid

for Carmen from Corpo Santo, who brought me up

Centuries ago, mother, in Delft (remember?)
you were tipping the jug in the home of Johannes
Vermeer, the painter, husband of Catharina Bolnes,
daughter of Mrs Maria Thins, that uptight lady,
who had a half-crazy son,
Willem, if my memory does not fail me,
who dishonoured poor Mary Gerrits,
the maid now opening the door
for you, mother, to enter
and go to the table in the corner
and from the jug pour the luminous butterflies
your family's cattle grazed
in Delft's green, sombre rags.
Just as I dreamt it in the Rijksmuseum,
Johannes Vermeer with milk will whitewash
those walls, the brass, the wicker, the bread,
your arms,
though in the fiction of the painting
the source of light is the window.
Vermeer's light, that enigma of centuries,
that ineffable clarity shaken from God's hands,
milk drawn by you in the dark shed,
in the bats' hour.

Red Rose, Proud Rose, Sad Rose

I knew some men who carried the red flag
when it was a sin and beautiful
like a holly berry.
I myself held one, a red flag, in my hands
when it was a sin and beautiful
like a stork's beak.
I've heard of men in Calcutta and Soweto
who still carry red flags,
beautiful like camellias between the teeth.
But I didn't want today to tell you
of the proud, red and sad flag
that heated the hands of those underneath,
a sin and beautiful like a coal flame.
I only wanted to tell
of the holly berry,
the stork's beak,
the camellia between the teeth,
the coal flame
and the proud, red, sad Rose of Yeats.

The Last Judgement

> *Riseth ye up that ben ded, and cometh to the jugement*
> Chaucer

And so God will send the angels
to separate the good from the bad.
And they will put some to one side with Saint Abel,
the martyrs
and the beggar Lazarus.
The others with Cain,
the blustering tyrant
and the rich glutton.
On the right Peter and on the left Judas
the infamous.
Till when? the damned will ask.
And the Lord will clear his throat with a glass of water:
For ever and to the end.
And when everything's over,
we'll arrive,
the latecomers,
a Soneira cart moaning
in the now deserted valley of Jehoshaphat.

Hearth

Come with us, winter,
orphan of many,
come next to the cold,
world inside the fire.

Tenderness

Seeing man on his own,
weary,
his hoofs in the snow,
ermined in stars,
howling towards the infinite.

A Man

He learnt to write on military service.
The line of his signature
scratches like a nail ploughing the ice on a tractor's windscreen.
He is made nervous by the telephone,
that stranger who enters without knocking,
in city shoes,
and is not smelt by the dog.
As for talking, he talks very little.
Life ate all his words
while making his hands bigger.
Those hands dug wells and held up roofs.
In such circumstances it's better to keep your mouth firmly closed.
But even like this he can't watch the killing of the pig,
the only meat he likes, especially if it's roasted.
Wine has to be cheap
and then, when he drinks it in long draughts,
I think it helps him swallow
a story he will never tell.
When he gazes at the fire burning in the hearth,
he travels on a train across the snow.
I'd take his hand, for he's my father,
but he is amazed as much by signs of affection
as by the air of a wolf.

Botanic Garden

There was a rose with black velvet
on the edge of its petals
and the gardener called it Lili Marlene.
One that flowered like a sin of the flesh
on June 16
was Molly, the Bloomsday rose.
But to the one he secretly loved,
its first fragrance,
he gave the name Moulin Rouge.

Snooker at the Royal Oak

Two pints on the bar,
distilled beer of the unfathomable night
with a gallon of fine lingerie.
Seven yellow balls.
Seven red.
One black.
Another, white.
Two cues
of the best oak in Eire.
This game began before the river Liffey was born.
There are some who don't know who's playing.
But I do.
And I don't flag.

Unforeseen Destiny

How ironic to end up at the last stop.
Indecipherable sign,
clock without hands,
frozen effigies,
heavy eyelids
and the old woman waxing the night on the station floor.
The stage was set for the arrival of a mistaken man.

Graveyard

It was at the burial of Antón Avilés de Taramancos,
in the parish of Boa.
He'll like the place, it has a good view,
said the little old woman with red eyes
when the earth rapped on the coffin.
Who said the people don't recognise their poets?

One Eleven

I'm in bed with the children, watching a film, *Numa the Killer Whale*. I'd spend the whole morning with them in this bed, noting the changes in heat: they go for some satsumas in bare feet, which I then warm between my thighs. It's Sunday. Through the window the white belt of frost girdles the river Small Valley. Later, in the winter sun, the fields seethe with an animal breath. Like golden lingerie, the candles in Somonte blossom. We visit Frixe, a little country Romanesque church surrounded by a cemetery with lots of cement niches (and four left in stone, perhaps in an act of mercy). There can't be so many dead from now to the end of the world. The boy's attention is drawn to the name *Palmira* engraved on one of the black marble slabs. The path to Nemiña Beach is no longer lined with those dramatically twisted posts that seemed to have emerged from an ancient pilgrimage along the deep sea lanes. They're now straight, solid, concrete posts, uniform in nature, that the eyes end up ignoring. The charm of this world has something to do with the extreme fragility of the shore in contrast to the roughness of the sea and the powerful wings of the great heavenly bird. Next to a boat, the children find a lesser-spotted dogfish half buried in the sand. It's a thin ocean muscle, miraculously still showing signs of life. When it turns, it contorts its arm in agony. I run with it towards the sea. It smells of salty blood, and gapes. I can see fear and hope in its dark eyes. We throw it from the rocks, carpeted with tiny mussels. The currents drag it back towards the beach, but it gradually regains strength and tries to reach the open sea, impelled by our desire. We lose sight of it in a turbulent blue embrace.

One Twelve

On the A552, at the turning for Transurfe, we head for Coucieiro and from there for Castro. We start walking and, on the path leading to the waterfalls and the river's cauldrons, come across an abandoned chapel, a beautiful piece in this ancient kingdom of melancholy. Nobody was able to remove the stone reredos; the roof of the apse is made with slabs of stone, home to a thriving laurel. The rest of the church is open; ivies crown the façade in an arch. The walls are watercoloured with lichen. They say that lichen, that association of alga and fungus, can take a hundred years to cover the palm of a hand. The chapel must sometimes serve as a sty because it's littered with manure. Somebody has made a lean-to with Uralite for a tractor that seems not to have moved in years and shares the garage with old country cart-wheels. A local informs us that the chapel is in honour of Saint Eutel. Saint who? Saint Eutel. And then mutters something about what do we care for their neglected saint. We head down paths of gorse to the waterfall. Right at the top there's a tiny mill, small like a hut in a Japanese garden. The waterfall carves out cauldrons overflowing with foam. The mountain slopes damming the rivers are a succession of superimposed slabs, like two enormous natural dolmens. The water is so cold your hands burn as soon as you wet them. Milady, the grey wagtail, leaps from stone to stone.

One Sixteen

The homeless took a step out on to the sea of clouds and fell from Caspar David Friedrich's painting. As he went down the Underground steps, in the frozen night, he carried Van Gogh's bed in Arles on his back.

One Seventeen

The fascination of things in the hands. Things have life in the hands. The age of the nut. Knives, gigantic ridges of imps. The wooden mallet, a dull thud that opens the nut and out comes winter's cerebrum, the snowman's brains. Night's street lights on the wet roads, the moon's clove of garlic, throwback of the sun now shining on Borneo. The hands turn the dial. Short-wave band 5 at 23:15, Radio Moscow International talks about the Russian Orthodox patriarch and an avalanche of snow in the Urals. An avalanche is too big for the hands. The cerebrum directs the hands, the hands grasp things, things seduce the hands, the hands stroke the cerebrum's moss and navelwort. Two men were working in the new cemetery. What do you feel when you build a cemetery? They seemed happy enough when I looked. Then it started to rain and they each got in a niche. *At The Voice of Galicia*'s offices in Carballo, Ameixeiras introduced me to a hunter. He was a young, blond boy with acne. He told me he had seen a heron and not fired. The trigger tickling the fingers. The eyes following the heron's grey and crested whiteness. The yellow beak pecking at the snow's brains. Letting it go, that *coup de grâce*. I turn the dial. Music of dervishes. Just three dance steps to the window and I open the plates of the Book of Heaven.

Statistic

The biggest kissers:
fish.
Followed by the wild canary.

Message

The pebble he threw on Nemiña Beach
bounced three times
and three waves encircled Isabel on Havana Pier.

The River

From the other side, Lord, I see this green
and these fertile lands
and a stream with baskets of old gold
and a dovecot of messengers
and an angel husking ears of corn
next to a granary of a hundred feet.
I know I'll never cross that river
murmuring a farewell lament for me.
I'll stay in the mill's ruins,
stive whitening the windows of my eyes.
That's the pride I'll call destiny.
But I was one of yours, Lord.
You may still remember that other
who jumped over rose bushes after the call of bells
and thought he had written the poem of bread for you.
Our Father, therefore, which art in heaven,
in memory of the one I was,
tell the Rio Grande to play
that blues again.

New Romance of Fin Negan

The dark enigma that is me
Eduardo Pondal

I
IN RETREAT

Fin Negan is getting on the straight line of the plots
that is so perfect, so straight,
he doesn't find his steps
or cart-tracks
or hedges or fences
or laurels or anything at all,
false trail,
smooth and flat,
without pebbles or blasphemies,
without the carpet of pine needles on the paths,
without gargoyles of fear on the banks,
without pools of memory in the gullies,
an engineer's endless short cut
to get to the graveyard soon.
From cross to cross,
the barn owl carries the moon in its talons.
The boy stabbed in the red lantern
sticks a howl of honour in the night's jukebox.

And Fin Negan's dog also barks
the hymn of those left in the ditch.
A round for everyone!
He'd willingly invite everyone to a round,
but Fin Negan hasn't any loose change in his pocket,
shame about the tinkling in the bell of his throat.
Hey, company! Health and Home!
But then he spits tobacco crumbs:
Ah, lazy death!
Fin Negan is getting on,
waft of mist
that'll join the river,
Galicia's finest silk.

II
FIN NEGAN'S SON

A hunter of moths
was flying over the lights of Manhattan
when Fin Negan's son
came out of the Mehari Arms
in Vimianzo.
A boat ran aground on the Outer Sea
with a cargo of accordions.
A boat of oranges.
A boat of wild beasts
for London Zoo.
Metro Goldwyn Mayer's lion
was actually heading for the Phoenix Park
in Dublin.
It left its prints on Thirteen Beach.
Crossed Hanging Boulder Ridge.
Guided by the red star
of the relay station.
Climbed on to the cornerstone
of the green wall in Oil Lamp Street
and roared: Babylon the great is fallen, fallen!
From the Horses' Fountain
the hunter of beyonds examined

Soneira's twelve candelabra
and then accelerated down Ogas Straight.
Fin's son wanted to talk to his father
in Vilar Cemetery,
but was afraid he'd ask him about the dog.
The dead do such things!
So he called the early-morning show
on which bakers tell jokes
and security guards request love songs.
Fin Negan's son in a phone box.
MGM's lion having sniffed out Irroa's dreamy sheep.
The hunter of angels with a scanner.
Twenty-four elders on the accordion in the Porch of the Outer Sea.
To be continued…

III
THIS IS JOKER!

A joke. Tell us a joke.
Or sing something. A copla, a habanera,
a cumbia, a Mexican corrido.
Or even, if you prefer, a muiñeira.
Don't hold back, my friend.
The whole of Galicia is listening!
What did you eat today? Wait, don't tell me.
Peas, new potatoes,
Betanzos cabbage
and onions.
Ho, ho, ho. What joy!
This is Joker, king of the night,
cock that awakes the day.
I'm not happy about that silence.
Tell us something, anything.
Wag your tongue a bit.
This show's a party!
No jokes, no singing, no saying what you ate.
Why did you call, if you don't mind my asking?
At least tell us your name.
Fin Negan. Louder! Fin Negan!
Finally, ho, ho, we know something about the man.

IV
MY GALICIAN LAND

There's a hunter of beyonds around here.
Oh, really? You don't say!
A hunter of angels.
Explain that to us, Fin Negan. Make us laugh.
It's not a joke. A hunter of moths.
Right, Fin Negan, with a laser and dip-net.
No, he has a soul detector. He's coming for me.
Easy, my friend, we're with you. Ho, ho.
And there's a lion.
Sure, Fin Negan. Metro's lion.
Yes, on top of a green wall
in Oil Lamp Street.
You're an amusing guy, Fin Negan,
welcome to our club!
The lion's saying Babylon is fallen.
Fantastic information, ho, ho, let everybody know!
Where's Babylon?
Good question, Fin Negan. But where are you calling from?
(I don't know if I should.) From a phone box.
You must be somewhere! Trust me, my friend.
I wanted, I wanted a song
dedicated to my father.
Anything in particular?
Pucho Boedo, *My Galician Land*.
OK. Now tell me where you are.

and V
THE ENDING

Who was the painter with his brush that brought together
all the colour green on your skin?
Hi, Fin! Surprised?
Pucho Boedo. *My Galician Land.*
Who put in your line…?
Touching!
Come on now, don't keep me waiting.
Free that beyond, Fin Negan!
What's in your heart,
my Galician land?
Ho, ho, ho.
Free that beyond, Fin!
Free that angel!

Questions

I

My thanks to the organisers for inviting me
to this symposium on the avant-garde crisis.
Ladies and gentlemen:
Allan Poe used to say that the machine-gun...
In that phase of the arms race,
you could be a Suprematist, Futurist, Dadaist, Surrealist,
Constructivist and even an Optimist,
although Kazimir Malevich already painted
the black square a second time
and Vladimir Makovsky gave the quartermaster-sergeant
back his uniform,
albeit missing the beret with the red star of hope
that served as a target
in the position of farewell.
The imagination of starlings changed with Guernica.
Before that, they flew in an instinctive flock,
gracefully drawing the protective dream
of a powerful bird
frightening off the real.

Shortly afterwards, the industrial production
of death began.
Günther Anders recalls the harmless appearance
of the tins of Zyklon B in Auschwitz.
He also remembers how he made a fool of himself in France,
among cultured people,
when he predicted that this clown, Hitler,
refused admittance into Vienna's Academy of Fine Arts,
would bring unprecedented horror.
Under the moral obligation to hate,
Anders, in his own words,
had become a dark man,
a queer fish,
but managed to write a book of denunciation.
In New England,
somewhere on Mount Washington,
Günther Anders
sat down at the foot of a walnut tree
with a notebook in his hand.
He didn't discover the nut of gravity,
but instead a question I now pass on to you:
Why?

II

Men who have ascended Everest
have reacted in different ways,
but almost all have given thanks to God,
stuck their country's flag in the summit
and taken photographs with an icy smile.
Were there a lavatory door,
we'd have more spontaneous messages,
of the kind: It's raining, it's snowing,
shake it before going.
Or else: From up here,
God,
you can't see a bloody thing.

III

That film, *Independence Day*, was laughable
because the invaders were monsters,
an irritating version of pock-marked,
Walt Disney octopuses.
Fear, real fear,
comes when the extraterrestrials are
intelligent men
who give themselves away
because they don't have tears
and don't appreciate bitter tastes
such as wine.
In five thousand million years,
the sun will be one of those withered stars
called red giants,
it'll throw up a demon
and the earth, they say, will burst like a bauble.
Somewhere
an invader with tears
will drink slightly acidic wine
and ask the dregs who he is.

Graffiti

Whoever you are, listen on this stone to the soul I was.
A happy man when he fashioned the Apocalypse in Mateo's
workshop. And the three ponies of the Adoration.
And the siren bird in the great choir, with a face I dreamed as it
emerged with a thousand and a hundred thousand burin kisses.
The chisel combed her long locks.
All my life I felt the embrace of her wings.
And she had four legs:
a she-wolf's, a wild cow's.
She was hot inside like stone.

Whoever you are, you may not know that stone is hot.
Like the mountain.
Her eyes are green. Golden in the west.
Stone burns the hands in a night-blue flame.
Like the mountain, she has berry, dragon-red blood.
I'm grateful to stone for the love she gave me.
The warmth, the company, in the cold hell of my days.

Whoever you are, you may not know that stone speaks.
Related everything you see now.
Conquered death, eternal peace.
Taught me this language the wind doesn't carry off.

Whoever you are, I was a friend of hers.
Don't let guilt or pity hold you back.
Read me aloud.
I only want to hear from your mouth what I was.
Whoever you are, I was a friend of hers.
A stonemason in Compostela I was.
I was her friend, a friend of hers.

The Singer's Beret

My beret on the street floor is the Bank of Europe.
Please do not throw sadness in my cap.
I'm not asking you for a pair of eyes.
I'm not a beggar.
I dig in your pocket with my song.
I sing like an out-of-work Welsh miner,
like a peasant catching the last train in Europe
in search of the ram with wings and golden fleece.
My cap, my brimless hat, is my castle, my country, my mobile.
Loosen your hands!
Free the swallows!
Let your coins show their mitre.
Throw in at least the cost of a European missed call.
I have to make a phone call to my childhood.
Children adore money.
I remember the earthy smell of my first wage.
We helped collect potatoes.
Felipe's dad gave us a silver-coloured coin,
a peso or 5 pesetas.
It glinted in our grubby hands,
but we went and bought chromos of footballers.
Another day,

an old woman, Celia the fishwife, called me over:
Hey, boy! Go to the shop, will you, and buy some red wine
and a bun.
I pulled the same one as Jesus in Cana.
The fat, beached fishwife
gave me a coin smelling of the sea.
But under the scales
I again found the portrait of that ugly man,
Franco was his name.
Back then,
I was crazy about Cassius Clay.
I'd like to mint my own coins
with the boxer's face
or the visage of Marisol,
the girl I loved.
Once my grandfather said to me:
Listen! Always, always carry money in your pocket.
Money is very important for poor people.
The rich never carry small change.
He told the truth.
He wasn't a Euro-sceptic,
he was a World-sceptic,
but kept a pennyworth of hope in his beret.
Another time, he made this ironic prophecy:
There won't be a last judgement. Shame!
My cap on the pavement is a merry-go-round.

I know the price of silence.
The bitter, awful price of silence.
That's why I sing and sing and sing
on the cold corner of Europe Street.

> Previously broadcast by the BBC during a special
> programme to mark the introduction of the euro

One Missed Call

There it is, it's you, in an inner ring.
I repeat position:
Golf Alpha Lima India Charlie India Alpha
Though I think you,
precisely you, who'd have thought,
have a little hope.
There's a neon sign in your eyes.
Neon belongs to the avant-garde of hope.
Remember?
The message was:
Foxtrot Romeo Echo Echo Delta Oscar Mike
The photographs squeezed the light's jazz.
The lovers swayed
on a French accordion.
The neon shone
with the memory of a river
between the paving-stones.
The kisses were long.
The trams and boats
got lost in them.
What was the message?
Lima Oscar Victor Echo

Again:
Lima Oscar Victor Echo
And the unsettled parents vomited the electricity bill,
steakless boxers in the corridors of night night.
Since then,
I've noticed you have a little hope,
a hummingbird of hope,
a scrap of rainbow in the eye
like fishermen from Finisterre,
a firemouth.
I repeat position:
Golf Alpha Lima India Charlie India Alpha
In the inner ring,
emitting for an outer system.
What's the message? Over.
What's the message?

Prayer

The most profane was the one who believed most.
I recall that beggar's sneer
shooting the devout curse
awry.
Were stones to speak,
as Luke wanted,
they'd have the same accuracy.
He was wrestling with God,
sparring
with the great champ.
On the third word,
he shattered the sky
and a scrap of twilight
blinded his vision.
For him it was my mother's coin
and my chisel of remembrance.
I also will try,
lift
my palm and chin
up high:
Stop this war,
I order you, Lord!

I already wrote a letter to the newspaper,
twenty lines of well-controlled flow,
in which I omitted what mattered to me most:
on May 18 will the Egyptian swallow
reach Reykjavik
as every year for centuries?
I also signed a manifesto
addressed to the president.
In sensible, meaning
sorely afflicted terms.
I called on peace with many people
and on my lips felt the tickling of the earth
of this word scurrying among the flowers
like a graveyard mouse.
You're my last hope, Lord,
taciturn God the Father.

I see the president addresses you with great confidence.
There are those who say you're in on it,
you're the capo, the boss, the Don,
the top of the tree.
Allow me to keep my distance.
I do not share such familiarity.
I only preserve an electron of faith,
that is the invisible crumb,
shame.

For reasons of publicity,
allow me to curse you from very low,
reeling down Shit Street,
also known as Verea do Polvorín,
my soul drowned in a carton of Don Simón wine,
while Isaiah,
good and a little tedious,
preaches to me from the other shore:
How come you fell,
light of the morning?

In the name of guilt,
in the name of sin,
in the name of the sticky fear
careening my bones,
I order you, Lord, to stop this war!

Published in the Spanish newspaper El Mundo
on the eve of the 2003 war in Iraq

Practical Guide

And among the apple trees
may you also
be welcome,
White Queen of Canada,
on a par with the Pippins' Queen.
Health and Home,
Granny Smith.
Greetings, Elstar.
Here comes Jersey Mac
with the Green Maiden.
Starking Delicious:
I fall at your feet.
I await gravity
with scarlet longing.
Welcome also to
Williams' Bon Chrétien,
the pear trees' gallant.
I'm with you,
Reine Claude d'Oullins
and Mirabelle de Nancy
with the red ribs.

May the blackbird,
gorged on cherry,
sing a purple song
in the arms of Schneider's Noire.
I lost
the one they called the Beauty,
the most stolen apple in Galicia's orchards.
Only the worm of splendour is left:
the memory of a forbidden laugh.

Brotherhood

for Luis Tosar

Who is woodcock's eye
and who radar of fear?

Who is able to live
in the forest's shroud,
in the earth's rag,
in the bright web?

Who is able to scan
the sea's fury,
who swings
in the empty cage?

Who is flower of salt
in the wound's blister?
Who breaks the day,
who snows in the crystal ball?

Who rows along,
who pastures the clouds,
who rhymes rain
on the skin of silence?

Who floats a smile
in bitter amber,
who puts laurel on the door
when they all close?

The Enemy's Rap

He's my enemy, mother,
who takes me to dance.
You should've seen him, pretty, pretty mother,
the lord of chance,
how well he takes to the dance,
my enemy, my love.

He's my danger, mother,
star of the will.
You should've seen him, praised be mother,
the lord of evil,
how he lights the dance,
my enemy, my every glance.

He's my laughter, mother,
won't let me retire.
You should've seen him, angry, angry mother,
the lord of desire,
how he dances the dance,
my enemy, my glance.

It's him serenading, mother.
Don't call the police.
You should've seen him, dear, dear mother,
one day in the east,
when the dance fades,
my enemy, my pain.

Throw him out, mother,
I don't want to see him.
Who takes me to dance.
Who takes me to dance,
there's no forgiving.
Who takes me to dance,
my enemy, my living.

INDEX OF TITLES / *FIRST LINES*

A Hot Coffee   73
A Man   82
A Thousand   51
Arzúa: Snowfall of '87   57
Atlantic Avenue   36

Babel   72
Ballad on the Western Beaches   23
Beirut   47
Blues   44
Botanic Garden   83
Brotherhood   118

Café   66
Can you hear me? I'm in a phone box   54
Castro de Elviña   21
Celtic Apocalypse   42
Childhood   69
Confession   74
Country Suicide   40
Cricket   67
Culture   59

Dakar   50
Dark Is Life, Dark Death   24

Farewell   34
Ferrol   27

Graffiti   106
Graveyard   86

Haiku   49
Hearth   80
Hunting   63

*I went down to hope
           and turned over autumn*   30
Incio   26

Joshua Slocum's Trip round the World   35

Letter to a Son   48
Lower Miño Days   31
Lyric   58

Madrid   75
Message   93
Mother Earth   39

Nationalism   71
New Romance of Fin Negan   95
New Zealand   68

Omen and Legend   43
On your skin of a boat   29
One Eleven   87
One Missed Call   111
One Seventeen   91
One Sixteen   90
One Twelve   89

Power   56
Practical Guide   116
Prayer   113
Promise   33

Questions   102

Radiophony   46
Red Rose, Proud Rose, Sad Rose   78

Serpent with Wings   19
Shadow   70
She accuses me of having no feelings   52
Snooker at the Royal Oak   84
Statistic   92
Stop   65
Story   64

Television   62
Tenderness   81
Terrorism   61
The Black Earth   45
The Enemy's Rap   120
The English Cemetery   16
The Last Judgement   79
The Lonely Seafarer's Song   37
The River   94
The Singer's Beret   108
The Wood's Army   *38*
To flee from so much natal love   15

Unforeseen Destiny   85

Vermeer's Milkmaid   77

Weight on the Head   41
Welcome   60
Widows of the Living   22

Yes, I'm still here   55

Manuel Rivas (Coruña, 1957) writes in the Galician language of north-west Spain. His work has been widely translated. His novels *The Carpenter's Pencil* and *In the Wilderness*, in *Jonathan Dunne*'s English translation, were nominated for the 2003 International IMPAC Award and the 2004 Oxford-Weidenfeld Translation Prize respectively. *The Carpenter's Pencil* and three of his short stories, *Butterfly's Tongue*, were made into films. He is an active environmental campaigner and a regular contributor to the Spanish newspaper *El País*.

Jonathan Dunne's translations from Bulgarian, Catalan, Galician and Spanish have been nominated for major prizes (most recently the 2009 Warwick Prize for Writing). He has written *The DNA of the English Language*, a study of word connections in English.

For an up-to-date list of our publications, please visit our website:
www.smallstations.com

www.ingramcontent.com/pod-product-compliance
Lightning Source LLC
Chambersburg PA
CBHW030943090426
42737CB00007B/523